Forest Animal Kingdom
Stress Relief
Adult Coloring Books

John Kaiwell

Published by PUBLISHING COMPANY in 2016
First edition: First printing
Illustrations and design © 2016 John Kaiwell

allcoloringbook.com

ISBN-13: 978-1537137193
ISBN-10: 1537137190

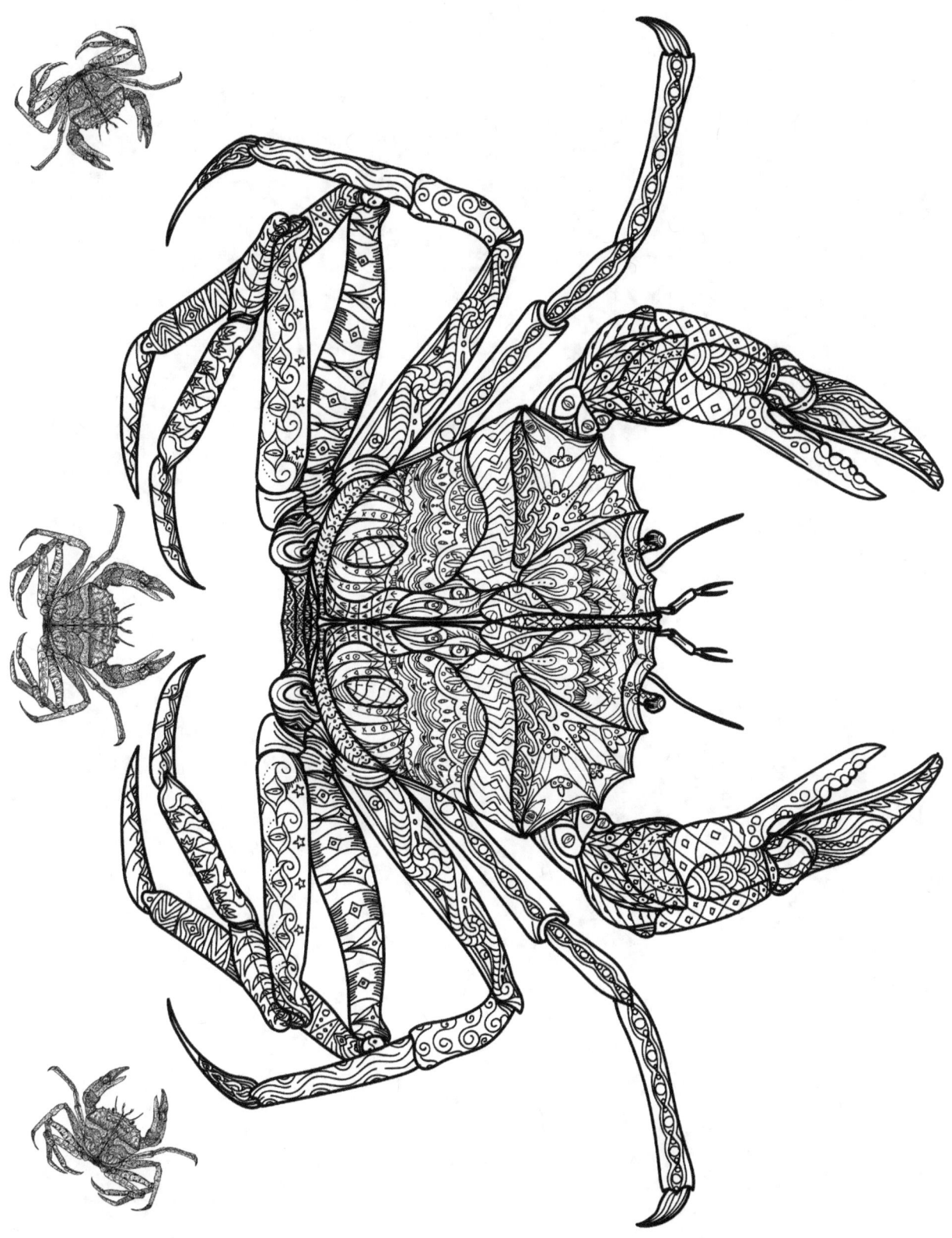

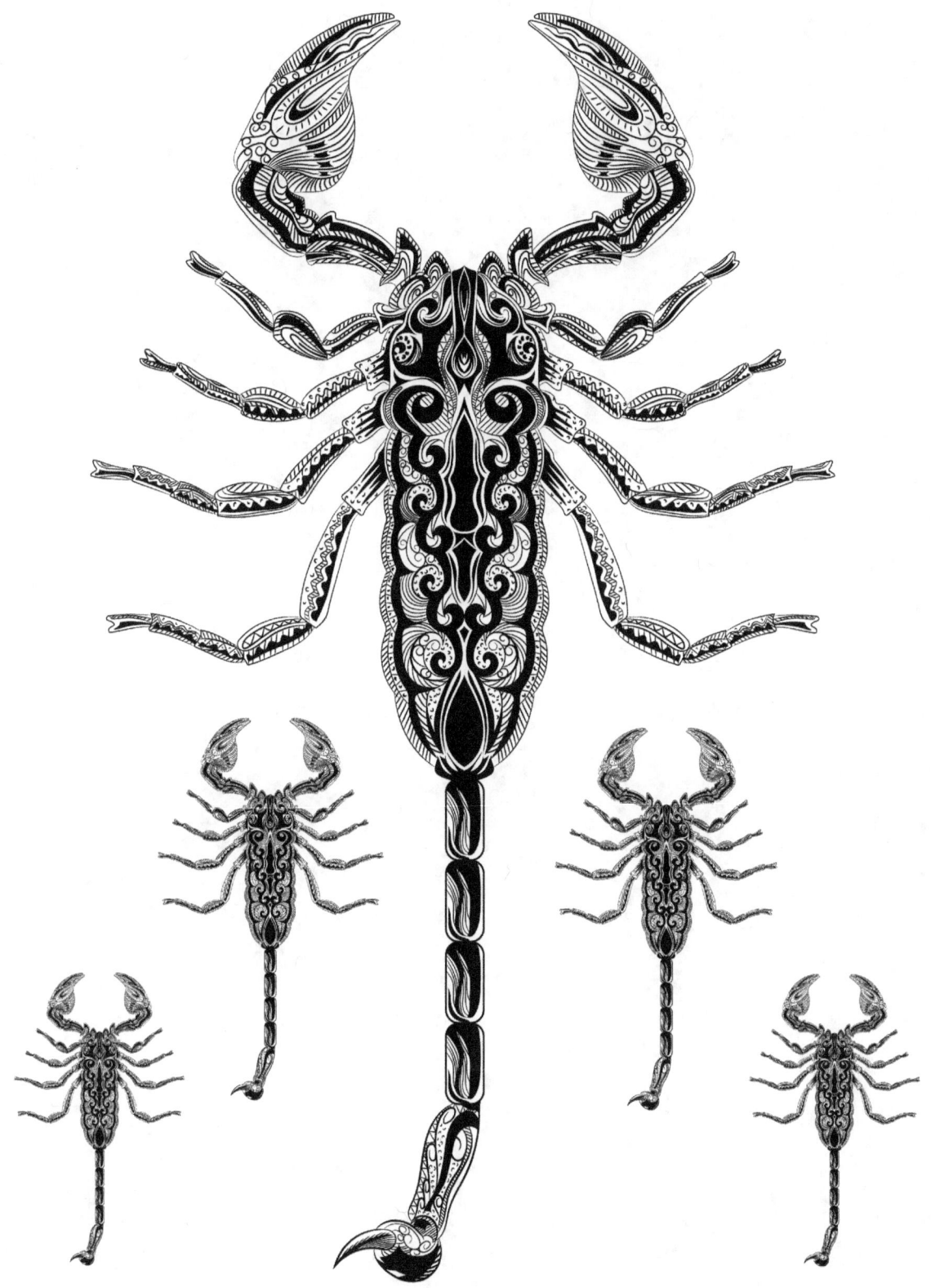

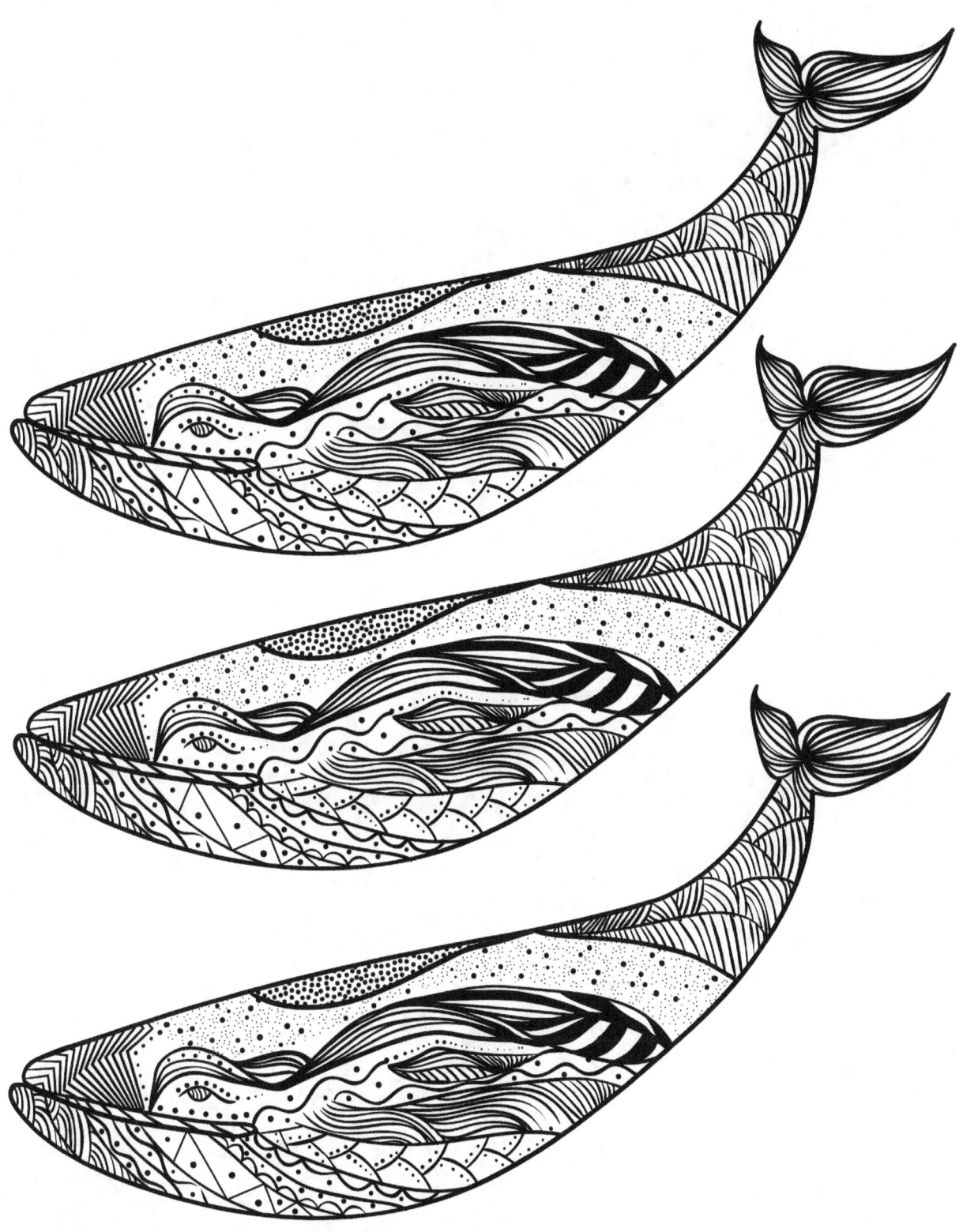

Thank You

Hope you've enjoyed your reading experience.

We here at Adult Coloring Book J. Kaiwell will always strive to deliver to you the highest quality guides.

So I'd like to thank you for supporting us and reading until the very end.

Before you go, would you mind leaving us a review on Amazon?

It will mean a lot to us and support us creating high quality guides for you in the future.

Thanks once again and here's where you can leave a review.

Warmly yours,
The Adult Coloring Book J. Kaiwell Team